MW00695554

LIST YOUR GOALS JOURNAL

LIST YOUR GOALS

Journal

100 Lists to Inspire and Motivate Your Growth

ERICA DIAMOND

ROCKRIDGE
PRESS

First Rockridge Press trade paperback edition 2022

Rockridge Press and the Rockridge Press logo are trademarks or registered trademarks of Callisto Media Inc. and/or its affiliates in the United States and other countries and may not be used without written permission.

For general information on our other products and services, please contact our Customer Care Department within the United States at (866) 744-2665, or outside the United States at (510) 253-0500.

Paperback ISBN: 978-1-68539-938-2

Manufactured in the United States of America

Cover Designer: Linda Snorina
Interior Designer: Kristina Spencer
Art Producer: Melissa Malinowsky
Editor: Brian Sweeting
Production Editor: Caroline Flanagan
Production Manager: Lanore Coloprisco

All illustrations used under license from Shutterstock; Author photo courtesy of Ryan Blau

10 9 8 7 6 5 4 3 2 1 0

This book belongs to:

_____

CONTENTS

INTRODUCTION **viii**

HOW TO USE THIS BOOK **xi**

PART 1
Goals for Personal Growth **1**

PART 2
Goals for Professional Growth **23**

PART 3
Goals for Healthy Habits **45**

PART 4
Goals for Relationships **67**

PART 5
Goals for Well-Being **89**

A FINAL WORD **110**

RESOURCES **112**

REFERENCES **114**

INTRODUCTION

Welcome to *List Your Goals Journal: 100 Lists to Inspire and Motivate Your Growth*. You are about to embark on an incredible experience, and I'm grateful that we can take that journey together.

My name is Erica Diamond, and I work as a certified life coach and certified yoga and meditation teacher. I've also worked as the weekly lifestyle and parenting correspondent for Global News for almost 10 years in Montreal, Canada. I am a professional speaker, host of the *Erica Diamond Podcast*, founder of Bliss Essential oils, and course creator of Busy to Bliss, a 30-day mindset transformational course for women. That may sound like a lot of different roles, but there is one unifying theme throughout: I help people create strategies to level up their daily well-being and achieve their goals.

I discovered the power of list journals as a young child. My wonderful mother, a therapist as well, taught me how to get ideas out of my head and onto paper as a safe way to problem-solve and express myself. Lists have helped me move through difficult times in my life with greater clarity and confidence. My clients and course students have used lists to manifest their big-picture dreams and goals, and my kids have worked through challenging situations by starting with written reflections and moving on to action plans.

By learning strategies to prioritize your self-care, you'll experience less stress, more calm, and greater joy every day.

List journaling, in case you're new to it, is a powerful way to work through a range of complicated feelings via goal-oriented processes. The act of answering thought-provoking guided questions and writing them all down in one place allows you to monitor your progress and growth.

Although a list journal will help guide, inspire, and motivate your growth, a medical professional should address any ongoing or debilitating feelings of depression or anxiety. This book is not a replacement for a therapist, medication, or medical treatment. There is no shame in seeking help when needed—doing so is a sign of strength and courage.

As you work through this journal, be kind to yourself. Try to offer yourself acceptance, compassion, and self-love. You're doing the best you can at any given moment, and that's enough. There is no "right" way to experience growth. Growth isn't linear—it isn't a straight line up, and it's often messy. Super successful people aren't superhuman at all; they have just used discipline to build positive habits, one at a time.

I invite you to come exactly as you are. You already have everything inside you to live a rich life full of joy and abundance. I wish you Godspeed on your journey—and speaking of journeys, as the Chinese proverb so eloquently states, "A journey of a thousand miles begins with a single step."

HOW TO USE THIS BOOK

This journal is for anyone who could use some inspiration and motivation to make changes, big and small. This book will help support you in identifying and achieving your most important goals for the year through 100 inspiring list journal prompts and empowering affirmations.

This book is divided into five prompt topics to help you create a full 360-degree life of purpose and passion: personal growth, professional growth, healthy habits, relationships, and well-being. I recommend that you work through all the sections; however, allow yourself flexibility to flip to specific sections or journal elements depending on your goals. If you need to invest more time and energy in certain areas now, it's perfectly fine to dive into those sections first. Supplementary resources at the end of this book offer additional support for your journey this year.

You may want to keep this book on your nightstand. A great approach is to carve out some time to reflect when the world is quiet—shortly after you awake and again when you're preparing for bed.

Remember, mindset shifts and habits don't happen overnight. Be patient with yourself.

As you get started, think of your life right now as a clean slate. Your canvas is blank, ready to be painted with the brightest colors of possibility. The beauty is in the now, in the present moment. You are about to live your best life, and a fresh start can feel sublime.

PART 1

Goals for Personal Growth

Feel proud knowing that you've invested in yourself—to learn, to grow, to connect and evolve, to let go of what isn't working for you in order to make room for new beginnings with limitless possibility. It may have taken you a while to realize that it's time for change, but you're here now.

In this section, we'll explore some personal goals that perhaps you've let fall by the wayside as life responsibilities got in the way. We'll start to formulate a plan to put you and your personal growth back at the top of your priority list. Sounds exciting, right? We'll examine some mindset blocks and limiting beliefs that have been holding you back from living a life of abundance and prosperity. You'll get clear on your vision for your own happiness and then create the action plan to start living it now.

Personal growth and development are a transformational process. It takes time to unlearn old habits and beliefs about ourselves and start to move toward a more abundant mindset.

The good news? You can course-correct at any time. You don't need a new calendar year or some other marker—you just need the willingness to do so. Let's get started!

Ask yourself, "What do I really want in life?" This question will help you clarify the direction you want to move in. List your "big picture" dream goals.

_____

_____

_____

_____

_____

_____

_____

_____

_____

_____

**I am strong, grounded, and powerful.
Everything I need to live a life of
abundance already resides within me.**

List the ways that your dream life compares to your existing life. (Examples: I wake up dreading going into work as I currently have a toxic boss and my dream would be to wake up fulfilled and self-employed, or I am lonely right now and my dream life would be to wake up next to my ideal partner.)

List the obstacles that are blocking you from attaining your goal or dream life. Writing about the blocks begins the unblocking process, and this concept is called "Name it to tame it." When we can name, we can begin to tame. (Examples: Fear of failure is holding me back from pursuing my passion, or my limited financial resources at the moment are preventing me from starting my own business.)

List the people who are your biggest inspirations. What about them inspires you? (Note: these may be living people you personally know, historical figures, or celebrities.)

List the activities that bring you joy and delight in your life.
(Examples: Throwing a Frisbee with a friend, going to a concert,
visiting a museum.)

List the activities and experiences that lead you to lose track of time and feel in flow.

_____

_____

_____

_____

_____

_____

_____

_____

_____

_____

_____

**I am worthy of a life of happiness,
peace, and prosperity. I am deserving
of all the gifts coming my way.**

We all have our own superpowers. Think about what you're doing when you feel the most confident in yourself. List your greatest superpowers and gifts to the world. (Examples: I am a talented public speaker, I am a skilled baker, I have an innate ability to connect deeply with others.)

List what you could do to nurture this superpower or talent and play up your strengths. (Example: I think I have strong leadership skills, so I will commit to stepping into that role more at work.)

List your current limiting beliefs about yourself. What negative thoughts often come up for you? Be honest with yourself. (Examples: I have no time or energy, I don't deserve happiness, I'm not a good parent, I'll never learn how to do this properly, I'm not as intelligent as so-and-so.)

List the challenging thoughts that counter those limiting beliefs—
encouraging words that you can repeat to yourself when those
negative thoughts surface. (Example: Susan made the same mis-
take as me last week and she easily laughed it off; I will learn from
this error and improve next time.) What would you tell a friend who
shared those same limiting beliefs with you? (Example: "Tom, if they
didn't like your work, they would have fired you by now—you are
worthy of your job.")

List the ways that your limiting beliefs have held you back from accomplishing your goals. (Examples: My limiting beliefs have held me back from leaving a job I disklike, leaving a relationship that doesn't serve me, living life to my full potential.)

**I wholly and deeply accept
myself just as I am.**

List the ways you ask for help when you need it. If you tend to avoid asking for help, what are some areas where you could use it? Who can you ask to help you right now?

List the times when you went out of your comfort zone. Note how you felt.

_____

_____

_____

_____

_____

_____

_____

_____

_____

_____

_____

_____

List some activities you can do to gently push yourself out of your comfort zone. These will help you grow your resilience and courage muscle as you step into your power.

List the ways you can stay positive and focused when others' opinions of you are voiced as negative or unfavorable.

List the ways that you're actively serving others in your life. How do you feel when you're helping others?

_____

_____

_____

_____

_____

_____

_____

_____

_____

_____

**No matter what others may think of me,
I love myself unconditionally. My gifts
are unique, and my potential for
success is infinite.**

List your biggest accomplishments in the past year and how you were able to achieve them.

List the mistakes you've made over the past year that you're ready to start to forgive yourself for.

List the things you're grateful for right now.

Fun reduces stress and allows for clearer decision-making. Always schedule time for play each week. List ideas of what "fun" means to you, and the different ways you can create more space for fun and play in your life. (Examples: Enroll in dance classes, go to an outdoor concert, take part in an adult treasure hunt with friends, roller-skate, ride a bike to a picnic in the park.)

I am ready to let go of what no longer serves me to make room for new possibilities.

PART 2

Goals for Professional Growth

In this section, you'll focus on getting unblocked and moving in the direction of your professional goals and dream job. What I know for sure after working with professionals from around the globe for over 20 years: You're never too old, and it's never too late to course-correct.

You'll find this section especially valuable if you're looking to change careers, grow professionally, or advance in your current company. As you work through the journal prompts, you'll see how closely related your personal growth (explored in part 1) and your professional growth are. These journal prompts dig deep, and you'll answer some thought-provoking questions, such as: What will happen if you *don't* make a move, and you stay stuck in a professionally unhappy place?

Some questions might feel difficult to answer at first, but once you start to "rip off the bandage," metaphorically speaking, and get to the heart of your desires, you can begin to create a road map for yourself to move forward with greater ease and clarity.

Professional growth often means venturing outside your comfort zone. This may look like learning new skills, asking for a raise, or even changing careers. Remember that you are worthy of days that stimulate you, that make good use of your talents, and that allow you to enjoy personal and professional success.

List the professional goals that you want to reach in the next 12 months, the next 5 years, and the next 10 years. What is the motivation behind these goals? (Consider writing down these goals and posting them in a visible spot.)

I balance my personal and professional life with ease and without resistance. My family life, relationships, and career coexist in harmony.

List five action steps you could take in the next 6 to 12 months that would start to propel you closer to your professional goals. Make sure to add these three action items to your calendar to ensure you work on them. (Examples: Complete my résumé, make a list of fifteen potential employers, attend four networking events.)

List five blocks, real or perceived, that are holding you back from attaining your professional goals. (Examples: Lack of funds to start my dream company, lack of confidence, need for further industry knowledge, certification is required.)

List one action item to perform for each of the five blocks that will guide you along your career path and help get you unstuck. (Example: If the block is lack of industry knowledge, the action item is to schedule time to perform market research in your desired field.)

List the necessary steps to take if your goal is to get a raise or promotion in your current job. (Skip this prompt if your goal is to leave your current employment.)

List how changing your profession or career path would change your life.

_____

_____

_____

_____

_____

_____

_____

_____

_____

_____

_____

_____

**My dream job is not a destination, but a journey.
I choose to enjoy the journey each step of
the way, as happiness is always within me.**

List how staying in your current profession would affect you.

List any career goals that you set for yourself this past year and then accomplished. If you didn't set or accomplish any, list what got in the way.

List your role models when it comes to your career. (Think: Whose job would you secretly love to have?)

_____

_____

_____

_____

_____

_____

_____

_____

_____

_____

I don't need anyone's approval to follow my dream path. My professional goals are mine to pursue. No one's opinion will dampen my momentum.

List the traits that you admire about these role models. What is it about their jobs that you desire? Specifically, what about your dream job or desired career excites you?

List the people around you (in proximity or virtually) who can serve as career mentors to you. How can you reach out to them to pick their brains or seek their guidance? What are some next steps?

List your dream job(s) when you were a child. Simply put, what did you want to be when you grew up?

List your proudest or most accomplished career moment and describe why. This prompt will get you thinking about your career "sweet spot."

List some frequent compliments you receive about your performance at work. Does this give you any direction or insight into how you can step more into your zone of genius?

List any topic that you can get up and speak to an audience about for about 30 minutes, without any notes.

List the ways you're making a difference in your current job/
profession.

_____

_____

_____

_____

_____

_____

_____

_____

_____

_____

**I can course-correct at any time. I am not
planted in any one job. I am not a tree—I can
move myself whenever I choose.**

List a few ways that you can accomplish your career goals in your current job (if possible). If this isn't possible, list the ways you can find meaning in your job until you transition to your desired career. (Hint: How can you bloom where you're planted?)

List the current daily work tasks you perform that play to your strengths and bring you joy. List the tasks that you know you do well. (Think: What do others come to you for advice about or often say you're good at?)

List your current daily tasks that feel the most challenging or mentally draining. Think of the tasks you dread doing or that you keep putting off. Next, list some ways to tackle them in order of priority or delegate them to someone else.

List how you would fill your days if earning money was not a concern, and then list the ways you can sprinkle a little more of this into your work life. (Examples: You would travel more, or volunteer at an animal shelter.)

I am intelligent, dynamic, and
driven, and my ideas are needed.
I can make a difference, and I am
an asset to any organization.

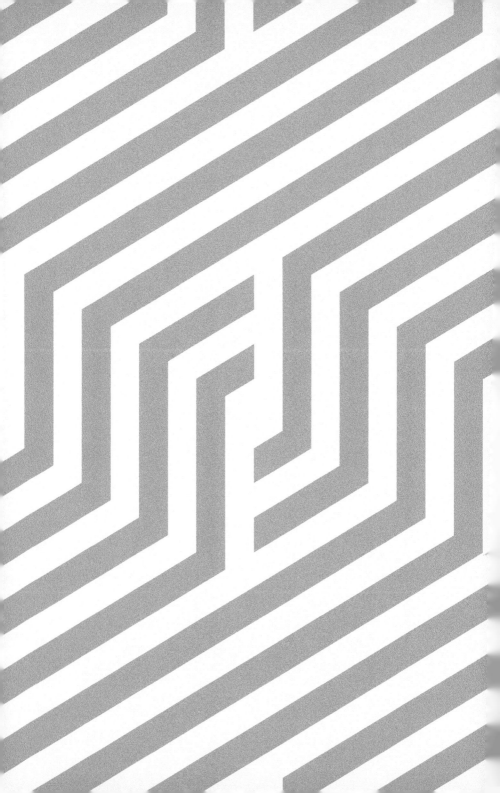

PART 3

Goals for Healthy Habits

In this section, you'll focus on creating new habits for your long-term health, well-being, and happiness. That might sound like a tall order, but once you begin to feel the physical and emotional benefits, you'll start to vibrate at a higher frequency—and others will start to notice it, too.

When setting health goals, keep in mind that the more *specific* and *measurable* they are, the better your chances of achieving them. Instead of writing "Eat more vegetables" in journal prompts, quantify it: "Eat five to eight servings of fruits and vegetables a day." This makes tracking your progress more manageable, and you'll feel a lot more in control.

Next, make sure that your goals are *realistic* and *attainable*. Unrealistic goals such as "I'll cut out all sugar for the next year" are much harder to sustain. You can't change your life overnight; the key to setting goals for healthy habits is to make small, manageable changes over time.

As you work through Goals for Healthy Habits, let's keep in mind one of my favorite quotes: "Optimist: someone who figures that taking a step backward after taking a step forward is not a disaster, it's more like a cha-cha." Expect a few cha-chas, setbacks, or bumps along the way. Growth is messy, as I've already shared. Expect the mess, and then reward yourself when you move through it.

You've got this.

List what your body would tell you if it could talk. Would it tell you that you need more sleep, healthier food, less screen time, or more self-care? Would it say it's proud of you? Be honest.

Without resistance, I release old habits that no longer serve me. I will create new healthy habits to make my days more abundant and joy-filled.

List the best pieces of health and wellness advice you've ever
received and how they helped you.

**I have the tenacity, strength, and perseverance
to follow the path to enhanced well-being.**

List the movements you enjoy doing. (Examples: Walking, running, dancing, biking, swimming, Zumba, yoga, Pilates.)

List the feelings you experience when you make time for movement. (Examples: Elevated mood, feeling healthier, having more energy, sleeping better.)

List and describe your morning routine. What changes could you make to start your day feeling calmer and more energized?

List and describe your bedtime routine. How could you design it so that you can conclude your day ready for optimal and restorative sleep?

List the ways you currently make time to meaningfully unplug so you can reconnect with yourself.

List the ways you can improve your boundaries around unplugging from all screens (TV, computer, phone, tablet). Then list ways that you can create healthier habits specifically around screen time.

List your favorite healthy foods.

List the foods that don't make you feel your best.

List your favorite nutritious recipes. When you're out of meal ideas, you can visit this list for inspiration.

_____

_____

_____

_____

_____

_____

_____

_____

_____

_____

I practice self-love and compassion on my journey to healing and creating habits that are better aligned with my values.

List your current hobbies and/or activities you'd like to try this year.

List the ways you make time for social connection, including groups of friends and family. (Examples: Night out with friends, mahjong group, date night, painting class, or book club.)

_____

_____

_____

_____

_____

_____

_____

_____

_____

_____

I surround myself with positive people who support my growth and development and who nurture me and hold me accountable.

List the ways you can organize the spaces in your home that are most cluttered. These spaces are often a representation of our cluttered minds. When we clean up—literally and figuratively—we can feel calmer in the chaos.

List any reasons you've neglected self-care and your health in the past. What is holding you back from living your best life now?

List some unhealthy ways that you currently handle stress—perhaps you overeat, bite your nails, or stay up late worrying. Then list some healthier alternatives. (Examples: I will take eight deep breaths, walk around the block, or read ten pages of a funny book.)

List one to three positive habits you can realistically commit to creating over the next 12 months. How will they serve your health?

_____

_____

_____

_____

_____

_____

_____

_____

_____

_____

_____

_____

List the ways that creating new healthy habits and leveling up your self-care regime will positively affect your personal and professional life. Reminding yourself why it's important to create a healthy life-style will help keep you on track.

List the challenges you'll encounter along the way as you replace unhealthy habits with more beneficial ones. Remember to be gentle with yourself as you work through these challenges of change.

List the ways you'll hold yourself accountable as you work through these challenges toward a more abundant lifestyle. (Examples: Create micro-goals, set a time line, track your progress, share your goals with a friend.)

My dream life is my responsibility to create. I am intentional. I don't just hope for a better life, I work for it.

PART 4

Goals for Relationships

This section is an important one. Even though the most important relationship in our lives is the one we have with ourselves, we still have to coexist and interact with other humans. When our relationships nurture us, support us, and fill our cups, our days are more fulfilled and joyful. When our relationships feel strained or difficult, an underlying feeling of heaviness and uneasiness can result.

In this section, we'll explore journal prompts and affirmations to strengthen the positive relationships we already have, and begin to shed those that aren't serving us.

So, how *do* you know if a relationship isn't serving you? How can you tell if a relationship is toxic or dark? For starters, do you notice that your mood takes a nosedive after you spend time with a particular person? Do you find yourself avoiding calls when someone's number appears on your phone? Those are a couple of red flags.

Perhaps you're on the fence about what to do with these people— whether to ditch 'em or keep 'em. Some relationships are harder to ditch than others—such as a boss. Through list journaling in this section, you can begin the unblocking process and determine who to hold on to and who to release.

List the people you consider your chosen family—also known as your "framily." These are friends who have become family.

_____

_____

_____

_____

_____

_____

_____

_____

_____

_____

My heart is soft, loving, and open. I form strong and meaningful relationships because I am able to let my guard down, and it allows me to be my authentic self.

List your deal breakers in friendships. What is it about these traits that lead you to run from a friendship instead of embracing it?

List the ways you give back to your community.

List how you think your closest friends would describe you.

List the people you rely on most for advice, feedback, direction, and support. (Hint: Think of the people you can *really* be your authentic self around.) What about them makes you value and lean on them?

List the ways you have allowed yourself to be open to forming new friendships or relationships over the past few years.

List the ways you have closed yourself off from forming new friendships or relationships over the past few years.

_____

_____

_____

_____

_____

_____

_____

_____

_____

_____

**I choose to always be kind first, and if someone
does not reciprocate that kindness, I will still
be okay. I know that if conflict does arise
along the way, I can do my part in helping
to resolve it quickly and with kindness.**

List how you are currently being supported in your closest relationships. Include notes on whether that is it enough for you and why or why not.

List the ways you can spend more time with the people you have the most satisfying relationships with. (Example: Making a standing breakfast date with your friend every 2 months on the calendar.)

List the ways you can create opportunities to meet new people who will lift you up and bring you joy, and whose values are in alignment with yours. (Examples: Attend networking events, join a gym, volunteer.) The Mayo Clinic found that volunteering benefits both physical and mental health.

List the energy vampires in your life. Who sucks the energy from you personally or professionally? What is it about them that drains your strength instead of fueling you?

List the ways you can distance yourself from the energy vampires or people in your life who feel critical of or negative to you.

I am deserving of real and authentic love and kindness from others. I love and accept myself wholeheartedly. My first love is self-love.

List the characteristics of an ideal friendship. Consider the traits that are important to you in any relationship. (Examples: Integrity, honesty, closeness, loyalty, kindness, and reciprocity.) Note why these are ideal traits. (Example: "They listen to me without judgment so I can be truly honest and problem-solve.")

List the person or people who inspire you to be a better person. Who is most supportive of your goals? Have you told them lately how much you appreciate them?

List your positive personality traits and qualities that you bring to your relationships.

List the ways you ask for help from those around you when you need it. Is it easy or difficult for you to ask for help? Why might this be?

_I communicate my needs openly and
honestly and with clarity and ease.
I understand that it isn't selfish to have
my needs met in my relationships._

List the ways you typically deal with conflict with colleagues, family members, friends, or others. (Examples: You keep your feelings to yourself, you prefer to talk to the person to resolve the problem, or you always shy away from confrontation.)

List the ways that you impose clear boundaries with those around you. (Examples: Not answering work calls after 6:30 p.m. on weeknights, unplugging on Sunday afternoons, or not lending money to someone who has not paid you back on a previous loan.)

List the ways that those around you are eroding boundaries. Try to be specific, and create a plan to present new firmer boundaries to them. (Example: You will no longer work overtime without pay, and you will schedule a meeting with your boss to discuss this.)

List the ways that you often say yes to people when you really want to say no. Then list how you can start to be firmer when you say no, reminding yourself that a no to someone else is a yes to yourself.

I am deserving of healthy boundaries in all my relationships. I can create boundaries that serve me well, and present them with confidence and ease.

PART 5

Goals for Well-Being

Welcome to our final part of this journey, where we'll focus on living a life of harmony and abundance.

Through your journal prompts and affirmations in this section, you'll create routines and rituals that support your well-being. You'll uncover old habits that have kept you feeling energetically low, and you'll find ways to create space for what sparks joy.

As we enter the final section, I'd like to remind you that growth is often uncomfortable. It certainly isn't linear, especially when it comes to our health and well-being. Remember the cha-cha? We go forward, then backward, then forward again. Change is also difficult. Most people do not welcome change. Sometimes change comes as a relief, especially if you're moving past a bad chapter in your life (divorce, leaving a toxic work environment), but it can also be very scary. Change can involve tremendous risk and often puts you outside your comfort zone. Creating new well-being habits just might mean assembling a whole new community and leaving those who don't support your goals.

It is the act of releasing old habits that no longer serve you and trading them for new practices that lead to happiness and well-being in your life. So, if happiness is found in your habits and lifestyle, then it is certainly within your reach. This means that you create your own happiness—and that is powerful.

Enjoy journaling about my favorite topic!

List your top ten favorite songs that put you in a great mood.

1. _____

2. _____

3. _____

4. _____

5. _____

6. _____

7. _____

8. _____

9. _____

10. _____

List what today would look like if it unfolded perfectly, just the way you like it.

List the activities or events that you are most looking forward to in the next few months.

List activities that calm you down when you're feeling upset or stressed. Think about what brings you the deepest sense of inner calm and peace. (Examples: Singing in the shower, knitting, playing Wordle, taking pictures, or calling your best friend.)

My body is healthy, my mind is calm, and I embrace a lifestyle that serves my total peace and well-being.

List the ways you can make more time for play in your life.
(Examples: Enroll in salsa dance lessons with a partner, join a book
club, plan an apple-picking outing, organize a bingo night with
friends, or go skating at the local rink.)

List the activities on your bucket list that you haven't tried yet.
(Examples: Bungee jumping, pole dancing, camping under the stars,
going to an amusement park, growing a vegetable garden.)

List what you did today to take care of yourself. (Example: Maybe you woke up early, made yourself a healthy breakfast and practiced yoga for 10 minutes, ate lunch outside without your phone, or created new work-related boundaries.)

List the ways you feel lucky in your life right now. (Examples: Your job is fulfilling and pays well, you have close friends, or your kids are all healthy.)

List your current habits, routines, or rituals that benefit your well-being. (Examples: You meditate each morning, make time for social connection, don't buy junk food, or sleep at least 7 hours a night.)

List some habits, routines, or rituals that are keeping you out of alignment. (Examples: You smoke, don't exercise consistently, eat lunch at your desk, don't unplug periodically, or aren't managing your debt properly thereby leading to stress.)

I unplug from technology easily. By unplugging and being present, I can embrace JOMO (joy of missing out) over FOMO (fear of missing out).

List some action steps that you can take to start ridding yourself of the habits that aren't serving you. (Examples: Sign up for a smoking cessation program, meal-prep on Sunday, or speak to a financial planner to start tackling debt.)

List the things you want to make time for every day. What are your well-being nonnegotiables? (Example: A 15-minute walk outside, a nightly bath, unplugging by 9:00 p.m., or taking an hour lunch break)

I ask for help with ease in my personal and professional life, freeing up my time and energy so I can live in alignment with my wellness values.

List your ten favorite places to go in your own city that lift your mood and keep you curious. (Examples: A favorite park, bookstore, café, or local museum.)

1. _____

2. _____

3. _____

4. _____

5. _____

6. _____

7. _____

8. _____

9. _____

10. _____

If you could redo your life, what would you do differently?

List the action steps that you could take that would make the biggest impact on your future well-being. Think about what your future self will be grateful for.

List any social media accounts that trigger jealousy or insecurity or that aren't in line with your values. How can you curate your feed for more inspiration and positivity, and unfollow those accounts that don't bring joy?

I am in total control of my happiness and well-being. My destiny is not managed by anyone other than me.

List what your inner critic says to you that keeps you feeling stuck or discouraged. (Examples: "I'm overweight," "I don't deserve happiness," "I'm not enough," "I'll never find time for self-care.")

List some positive and encouraging words you could say in response to your inner critic's voice. (Examples: "I'm learning to appreciate my body," "I'm worthy of a good life," "I am enough," "I will start making self-care a priority.")

List your five favorite inspiring quotes. Where can you post them to empower your well-being daily?

List some things you want to tell your future self. (Examples: "You will be okay," "You've got this," "Everything will work out for the best," "Don't forget to be present for your life.")

I trust the process of transformation. I don't rush it. There are no wrong paths, and I am on the journey for the long run.

A FINAL WORD

Congratulations! This was no small undertaking. Taking a 360-degree view of your life—and making a plan to keep doing what's working and changing up what isn't—takes great effort and is crucial to living your best life.

My hope is that this journal has inspired you not only to do the work, but to believe in yourself as you go. Stick with the goals you made for yourself in this journal, work on them each week, and you'll see results.

Consider keeping this journal on your nightstand as a reminder to work on yourself each day. Also, consider keeping a calendar nearby so you add self-improvement tasks to it as soon as they come to mind.

Keep in mind that it takes about 21 days to form a new habit, and anywhere between 66 days and 6 months for it to become more automatic. Should you veer off course on your journey, try to practice self-compassion. Remind yourself why you purchased this book, and then go back to your journal prompts. If you're struggling or feeling disconnected on your road to well-being, revisit the section you feel would be most helpful.

A good rule of thumb is to reassess your goals every 30 to 60 days. This is the sweet spot to implement change and then make any necessary adjustments. I like to use the first of each month to shift or tweak a plan.

I'm so grateful that you found this journal, however that came to be. I wish you bliss, peace, abundance, and fulfillment. Remember, you're right where you're meant to be, and you have everything already inside you to live a rich life full of joy and contentment.

And remember . . .

If you can't fly, then run.
If you can't run, then walk.
If you can't walk, then crawl,
But whatever you do, you have
to keep moving forward.

—MARTIN LUTHER KING JR.

RESOURCES

Author Resources

BlissEssential.co—Premium essential oil blends to enhance daily wellness and self-care.

BusyToBliss.com digital course—The 30-day mindset and body transformation for busy women who want to reclaim their time and energy

EricaDiamond.com—Private life coaching, yoga, and meditation sessions for well-being and resource articles for daily motivation and empowerment.

Erica Diamond Podcast—Getting you motivated and inspired by conversations with today's thought leaders and coolest people. Each episode, get up close and personal with compelling guests who share stories and tips that empower you to live your best life.

Podcasts

The Daily Boost, The GaryVeeAudio Experience, The Good Life Project, The Habit Coach, Happier, The Happiness Lab, Oprah Supre Soul Sunday Sessions, School of Greatness, TED Radio Hour, The Tim Ferriss Show, We Can Do Hard Things

Goal Tracker Apps

aTracker, Coach.me, Habitica, Habitify, Strides, Way of Life

Fitness/Movement Apps

FitOn, Glo, Le Sweat TV, MyFitnessPal, Nike Training Club, Runkeeper, Sweat, Sworkit, Yoga

Meditation/Mindfulness Apps

Aura, Breethe, Buddhify, Calm, Chopra, Headspace, Insight Timer, The Mindfulness App, Unplug, Waking Up

Books

The 4 Disciplines of Execution: Achieving Your Wildly Important Goals by Sean Covey, Chris McChesney, and Jim Huling

Atomic Habits by James Clear

Get Out of Your Own Way by Mark Goulston and Philip Goldberg

S.M.A.R.T. Goals Made Simple by S. J. Scott

Tiny Habits: The Small Changes That Change Everything by BJ Fogg

Your Best Year Ever by Michael Hyatt

REFERENCES

Maloney, Laura. "Council Post: How Reassessing Unmet Goals Can Uncover Your True Path to Success." *Forbes*. February 13, 2020. forbes.com/sites/forbescoachescouncil/2020/02/13 /how-reassessing-unmet-goals-can-uncover-your-true-path -to-success/?sh=65cd557d6bfd.

Mayo Clinic. "Helping People, Changing Lives: 3 Health Benefits of Volunteering." September 16, 2021. mayoclinichealth system.org/hometown-health/speaking-of-health/3-health -benefits-of-volunteering

ACKNOWLEDGMENTS

I want to acknowledge the many incredibly supportive people who have stood by me throughout my long and winding journey: my parents, my family, my friends, my online community. It takes, after all, a village to raise a *woman*.

This book is dedicated to my husband, Hilly, and two boys. My last book was written exactly 12 years ago, and the reason is no mystery—any spare moments I had over the past decade, I poured into raising my sons. Thank you for encouraging me to *finally* write this book and continue my life's mission to help as many people as possible manifest their personal and professional goals.

A special thank-you to my editors, Brian and Julie. This book is richer having had you both as a part of it.

ABOUT THE AUTHOR

Teaching busy individuals how to prioritize self-care, ERICA DIAMOND is a certified life coach and certified yoga and meditation teacher, lifestyle and parenting correspondent on Global News, professional speaker, host of *The Erica Diamond Podcast*, course creator of Busy To Bliss (BusyToBliss.com), founder of Bliss Essential (BlissEssential.co), author, and editor-in-chief of the award-winning lifestyle platform EricaDiamond.com (previously WomenOnTheFence.com).

Erica has been named to the coveted list of The Top 20 Women in Canada, *Forbes*'s Top 100 Sites for Women, and a Profit Hot 50 Canadian Company. Erica is a die-hard music lover and a busy mom of two teen boys.

CPSIA information can be obtained
at www.ICGtesting.com
Printed in the USA
JSHW050016230822
29359JS00002BA/2